THE NEW CALVINISTS

The New Calvinists
Changing the Gospel

E. S. Williams

THE WAKEMAN TRUST, LONDON
& BELMONT HOUSE PUBLISHING

THE NEW CALVINISTS
© E. S. Williams, 2014

THE WAKEMAN TRUST & BELMONT HOUSE PUBLISHING
(Wakeman Trust is a UK Registered Charity)

Wakeman Trust UK Registered Office
38 Walcot Square
London SE11 4TZ

Wakeman Trust USA Office
300 Artino Drive
Oberlin, OH 44074-1263

Website: www.wakemantrust.org

Belmont House Publishing
36 The Crescent
Belmont
Sutton SM2 6BJ

Website: www.belmonthouse.co.uk

ISBN 978 1 908919 32 8

Cover design by Andrew Owen

Printed by Stephens & George, Merthyr Tydfil, UK

Contents

1
The Phenomenon of New Calvinism
The Resurgence of Worldly Christianity

NEW CALVINISM is a movement that is sweeping across congregations in the USA and the UK, and other countries around the world. It has been described as a resurgence of the reformed teachings of John Calvin, and luminaries such as Jonathan Edwards. It has been called 'a growing perspective within conservative evangelicalism that embraces the fundamentals of 16th-century Calvinism while also trying to be relevant in the present-day world'.[1]

Led by very well-known names in the evangelical world, it plausibly gives the appearance of doctrinal soundness, but on closer examination we see a movement that dramatically changes how we live our Christian lives. It challenges the view of nearly twenty centuries of church history – that believers should be separate from the world. For the New Calvinism promotes full involvement in the pursuits of the world, bringing the world into the church in worship and witness, and eroding the difference between the holy and the profane. It is for the sake of individual Christians and churches that we should be aware of seriously harmful aspects of a movement that appears to be so promising. From the evidence presented in this book, we shall see that the problem of New Calvinism lies in both doctrine and conduct, and especially in conduct.

The apparent success of New Calvinism arises from a number of influential ministries, some associated with mega-churches, whose leaders are willing to work with one another. This cooperation has speedily affected the evangelical landscape. Such is its influence that even *Time* magazine, the world's largest circulation weekly news magazine, has noticed its impact on the evangelical world, placing it third on their list of 'ten ideas changing the world right now'. That was in 2009. It would be wrong to think of New Calvinism as founded on a clear doctrinal stand, for, as we shall see, it is a broad tent, with an assortment of different ideas, teachings, practices and doctrines. First we will look at the origin of New Calvinism and its association with The Gospel Coalition; then we will meet three American ministers who stand at the heart of New Calvinism, namely Dr Tim Keller, Pastor of Redeemer Presbyterian Church, New York; Dr John Piper, former pastor of Bethlehem Baptist Church, Minneapolis, and director of *Desiring God Ministries*; and Pastor Mark Driscoll, of Mars Hill Church in Seattle, who is reputed to be the most downloaded pastor in history. While the term 'New Calvinism' is seldom used in the UK, its underlying philosophy is being keenly adopted by churches and organisations here (as we shall see in later chapters).

The distinctive identity of New Calvinism first came to public notice in 2006, when Collin Hansen, then a junior editor of *Christianity Today*, published an article describing what he believed was a revival of reformed theology taking place among young Christians in the USA. He formed this conclusion after travelling around the country, visiting churches and institutions, and talking with theologians, pastors, and churchgoers.

Collin Hansen's book, *Young, Restless, Reformed, A Journalist's Journey with the New Calvinists*, published in 2008, tells the story of a calvinistic resurgence in the USA. Hansen was greatly impressed by the *Passion Conference*, a large annual event based on contemporary worship, with John Piper as keynote speaker. Twenty thousand students (far more now) who enjoyed modern praise music, gathered to hear Piper's reformed message. Dr Piper approved of the songs and told how they 'set the stage for the theology'.[2]

Collin Hansen wrote that in Piper's preaching and the music of the *Passion Conference*, young people were experiencing the nearness of God. 'This powerful combination at conferences like *Passion* blows apart stereotypes of reformed theology as a cold and detached study of God.'[3] He observed that, as evangelical Christians graduated from high school and left the church of their youth, many ended up at contemporary worship conferences like *Passion* or *New Attitude*, and were transformed by the music, and by the view of God they gained from the reformed theology of John Piper and others.[4]

Next in his journey Collin Hansen discovered that churches of a charismatic denomination named Sovereign Grace Ministries had united charismatic worship with calvinistic theology. He concluded that this 'growing network of charismatic Calvinists led by C. J. Mahaney is one sure sign of the reformed resurgence. Such a combination would have been unthinkable just a few decades ago.'[5] Indeed, he noted, so profound was the influence of C. J. Mahaney that his charismatic teaching was being widely accepted by New Calvinists. Hansen gave examples of this charismatic infiltration into reformed churches: 'More than a few people have been surprised to see [John] MacArthur, a cessationist, participate with Mahaney at the *Together for the Gospel Conference*. Even more worrying, he has invited Mahaney to speak at Grace Community Church and address pastors at the *Shepherds Conference*.' Hansen concluded, 'it's likely that reformed evangelicals will become more charismatic if Calvinism continues to spread.'[6]

He believed that a genuine religious revival was taking place, and made the following observations:

1) John Piper was the chief spokesman for the resurgence of Calvinism among young people.

2) Pastor Mark Driscoll of Mars Hill Church, Seattle, was a significant promoter of the new 'missional' emphasis of New Calvinism.

3) Al Mohler and the Southern Baptist Seminary in Louisville, Kentucky, were leading another renewal of Calvinism in the Southern Baptist Convention.

4) The *New Attitude Conference*, led by Joshua Harris and featuring reformed rap and rock music, was also reaching young people with New Calvinism.

5) New Calvinism had succeeded in combining traditional doctrine with the charismatic teaching and practice of C. J. Mahaney and the Sovereign Grace churches.

6) Tim Keller, of Redeemer Presbyterian Church, New York, was the leading cultural analyst of the New Calvinism.

Collin Hansen's book was extremely well received by many evangelicals. Pastor Tim Challies, well-known blogger, commented: 'Collin Hansen invites us on a voyage of discovery, learning how our restless youth are discovering anew the great doctrines of the Christian faith.' The editor-in-chief of *Christianity Today*, David Neff, was effusive in his praise: 'Collin Hansen has uncovered a fresh movement of young Christians for whom doctrine – particularly the Calvinist kind – fuels evangelism, kindles passion, and transforms lives. Read it and rejoice.'[7]

In the UK, Hansen's book was welcomed and reviewed with enthusiasm in well-known publications such as *Banner of Truth*, *Evangelical Times*, *Evangelicals Now* and *Reformation Today*. Later, The Gospel Coalition appointed Collin Hansen as their editorial director.

Dr Peter Masters, long-serving pastor of the Metropolitan Tabernacle in London (Spurgeon's church), expressed himself as deeply saddened to read Hansen's book. He said that 'it describes a seriously distorted Calvinism falling far, far short of an authentic life of obedience to a sovereign God. If this kind of Calvinism prospers, then genuine biblical piety will be under attack as never before... The author begins by describing the *Passion Conference* at Atlanta in 2007, where 21,000 young people revelled in contemporary music, and listened to speakers such as John Piper proclaiming calvinistic sentiments. And this picture is repeated many times through the book – large conferences being described at which the syncretism of worldly, sensation-stirring, high-decibel, rhythmic music, is mixed with calvinistic doctrine. We are told of thunderous music, thousands of raised hands, "Christian" hip-hop and rap lyrics...uniting the doctrines of grace with the immoral, drug-induced musical forms of worldly culture.'

Dr Peter Masters emphasised the point: 'You cannot have Puritan soteriology without Puritan sanctification. You should not entice people to calvinistic (or any) preaching by using worldly bait. We hope that young people in this movement will grasp the implications of the doctrines better than their teachers, and come away from the compromises. But there is a looming disaster in promoting this new form of Calvinism.'[8]

The influence of New Calvinism

We must appreciate that the influence of New Calvinism is worldwide, including Britain where its ideas and practices are rapidly gaining ground due to the influence of Tim Keller, John Piper and Mark Driscoll. Mark Driscoll is so well approved by evangelical leaders in the UK that he was invited to address the *London Men's Convention* in the Royal Albert Hall in 2011. Tim Keller has been strongly endorsed by the Proclamation Trust in the UK, having spoken at four annual conferences of their Evangelical Ministry Assembly (EMA). In 2011, he spoke on how contemporary preaching needed to be culturally contextualised, while rooted in orthodox Christianity. In simpler language, the Gospel must be made culturally acceptable, and in order to do so needs worldly methods to help it.

Charismatic practices and 'Emerging Church' ideas and practices, including mysticism, have found a home in the New Calvinism, including contemporary entertainment music in its most worldly forms.

To understand New Calvinism we shall examine the teaching of the three most influential leaders, already referred to. First, however, we need to look at The Gospel Coalition, an organisation in the USA at the forefront of New Calvinism.

The Gospel Coalition

Established in 2007, The Gospel Coalition is the brainchild of Dr Don Carson, Research Professor of New Testament at Trinity Evangelical Divinity School in America (who wrote its confessional statement), and of Dr Tim Keller (who produced its theological vision for ministry). Pastor Mark Driscoll was also involved in the founding of the Coalition. He was invited to attend a small theo-logical gathering, led by Carson and Keller, which also included men from a number of prominent American evangelical churches. Also represented were organisations such as the Council on Biblical Manhood and Womanhood, *Desiring God*, Together for the Gospel, the Alliance of Confessing Evangelicals, Sovereign Grace Ministries and ministries started by Mark Driscoll, namely the *Acts 29 Network* and *The Resurgence*.

The ambitious vision of The Gospel Coalition was to create a movement that by long-term effort would renew and reform evan-gelical thought and practice, both in the USA and worldwide. Collin Hansen writes about the first Coalition meeting: 'As Carson told me today, this group could not have come together five years ago. Make of that what you will, but something's stirring in the evangelical movement. The Gospel Coalition seeks nothing less than a return to the theological consensus enjoyed in the days of neo-evangelicalism, led by Billy Graham, Carl Henry, Harold John Ockenga, and many others.'[9]

A new social gospel

Among its prime aims The Gospel Coalition sought to motivate pastors and theologians to undertake social activity. Its theological vision for ministry would urge Christian people to become a counter-culture for the common good. The 'doing of justice and mercy' would become a highly important aspect of Gospel-centred ministry. It is claimed – 'The resurrection of Jesus shows that he is going to redeem both the spiritual and the material. Therefore God is concerned not only for the salvation of souls but also for the relief of poverty, hunger, and injustice.'[10]

Evangelical churches and missions have always shown immense compassion for the needy, but not as a mission equal to the spreading of the Gospel. The resurrection of Christ points to the perfection of the eternal hope. It is not a warrant for the promotion of a perfect society on earth. This view is none other than the old social gospel conceived by theological liberals and popular among them in the early twentieth century.*

A licence for worldliness

The Gospel Coalition is also concerned to revise the way the church relates to culture, which is referred to as the contextualisation issue. 'We believe that every expression of Christianity is necessarily and rightly contextualised, to some degree, to particular human culture; there is no such thing as a universal a-historical expression of Christianity…The Gospel itself holds the key to appropriate contextualisation.'[11] The Gospel Coalition warns that the Gospel may

---

* The notion of social restoration as Christ's purpose goes further than the *Neo*-Calvinism of Abraham Kuyper.

be 'over-contextualised' or 'under-contextualised', and so the aim of the church must be to get the right cultural 'balance' in presenting the Gospel. In short, the old, well-defined standards of separation from the world are obscured in the mist of pseudo-intellectual jargon, so that believers can be led into compromising flirtation with worldly methods.

Contemporary worship

The Gospel Coalition is completely given over to contemporary worship, and many Coalition conferences have included hip-hop concerts. An article by Collin Hansen, entitled 'The Hip-hop Opportunity', published on The Gospel Coalition website, describes a hip-hop concert held in the Moody Bible Institute: 'The auditorium pulsated with youthful energy for nearly three hours. A diverse crowd of nearly 2,000 had formed large lines long before the doors opened to general admission seating. During the sold-out concert, they shouted out familiar lines and danced with abandon among friends and new acquaintances who shared common affinity for the music. But the message took priority over the music and even the musicians on this evening. And that's just the way everyone wanted it…The concert – featuring rappers Lecrae, Trip Lee, Sho Baraka, Tedashi, Pro, and DJ Official – made Jesus Christ the star of the show.'[12]

An article in *Christianity Today* under the headline, 'Spotlight: Reformed Rap and Hip-hop', publicised the holy hip-hop movement. According to the article, holy hip-hop and Christian rap music have become closely associated with New Calvinism. The growing edge of the Christian rap movement 'is explicitly taking its cues from Calvinist leaders. Several tracks have included direct references to (and even sermon clips from) John MacArthur, John Piper, C. J. Mahaney, and other pastors, and Curtis "Voice" Allen's recent rap on the Westminster Catechism (with theologian D. A. Carson) went viral in March – as did his Heidelberg Catechism rap last October.'[13] One characteristic that most New Calvinists have in common is this devotion to so-called 'culturally sensitive' contemporary Christian worship. Most churches that follow the ways of New Calvinism will make use of a worship band with loud, rhythmic music.

New Evangelicalism

It is valuable to understand the relationship between New Evangelicalism and New Calvinism. New Evangelicalism, which developed in the 1940s and 50s, openly repudiated the beliefs of fundamentalists, and developed a more accommodating form of evangelicalism that did not practise separation from teachers of false doctrine. The theological leaders of the New Evangelicals were Dr Harold Ockenga, who probably coined the term, and Professor Carl Henry, both of whom played a key role in the founding of Fuller Theological Seminary in the USA. (By the middle of the 1960s Fuller Seminary was firmly in the hands of scholars who were clearly opposed to the doctrine of biblical inerrancy.) Fuller became the bastion of non-separating Christianity and the academic power-house of New Evangelicalism.

In 1956, with the support of evangelist Billy Graham, Professor Carl Henry began publication of *Christianity Today*, which became the voice of the New Evangelicals. It now seems to have evolved into the mouthpiece of New Calvinism.

New Evangelicalism and New Calvinism have much in common. Just as New Evangelicals had a low view of Scripture, taking on board many critical, liberal opinions (such as the renouncing of the days of creation, a global flood, and numerous other matters), so the New Calvinism includes those with a defective view of Scripture. Mark Driscoll and Tim Keller, for example, are frequently careless and irreverent in the way they use Scripture. Most have no respect for the fourth commandment as applying today. Most do not recognise the Bible as having real normative and practical authority over how Christians worship and order their churches.

New Evangelicalism compromised on the biblical command to separate from false doctrine, and was eager to form spiritual alliances with all who professed to be Christian, whatever their beliefs. They were soft on theological liberals and on the Church of Rome. They urged people to remain in doctrinally mixed and even dead denominations. In a similar way New Calvinists desire to work with charismatic and emerging churches, and wink at the adopting of Catholic and New Age mysticism. One of the most prominent features of New Evangelicalism was that it sought acceptance by the world, and strove for intellectual respectability. New Calvinism is even more openly worldly in its tastes and conduct. New Evangelicalism added an unduly prominent social activism to the work of the church, elevating this to rank alongside Gospel work. New Calvinism shares this seriously mistaken and unbiblical goal.

2
Tim Keller
The Intellectual Populist of New Calvinism

DR TIM KELLER is a conspicuous pillar of New Calvinism. As the senior pastor of Redeemer Presbyterian Church in New York, he claims to promote reformed Christianity. He is regarded by many as a great intellectual, and an expert in Christian apologetics. *Newsweek* has dubbed him 'the C. S. Lewis of the 21st century'. He is skilled in arguments that demonstrate the truth of the Christian faith in a postmodern world. In one of his sermons Tim Keller helps his listeners to see Jesus Christ as 'existentially satisfying' and 'intellectually credible'.

Tim Keller is a best-selling author as well as a popular conference speaker. He has written a number of books, including *The Reason for God* (2008), which reached the top ten on the *New York Times* list of best-sellers. He is so highly regarded in evangelical circles that he was a keynote speaker at the Third Lausanne Congress on World Evangelisation (2010) held in Cape Town, South Africa.

Under Tim Keller's leadership Redeemer Presbyterian Church has greatly prospered and now has approximately 5,000 members. Redeemer City to City is their worldwide church planting movement consisting of around 150 congregations throughout the USA, and in other countries. Those who join the church-planting movement are expected to propagate Tim Keller's philosophy, books, sermons and articles. However, despite Tim Keller's towering reputation and popularity among evangelical Christians, we need to examine carefully the total message that he preaches.

Tim Keller's background

In his book, *The Reason for God* (2008), Tim Keller speaks of his upbringing in the Christian faith. As a teenager in a Lutheran confirmation class, he was impressed with a teacher whom he describes as 'a social activist…filled with deep doubts about traditional Christian doctrine'.[1] From that teacher, he learned about a 'spirit of love in the universe, who mainly required that we work for human rights and the liberation of the oppressed'.[2]

In college he was 'heavily influenced by the neo-Marxist critical theory of the Frankfurt School'.* Tim Keller explains: 'In 1968, this was heady stuff. The social activism was particularly attractive, and the critique of American bourgeoisie society was compelling…'[3] He admits that he was 'emotionally' drawn to the social activism of the neo-Marxists. 'How could I turn back to the kind of orthodox

---

* The Frankfurt School, to which Tim Keller refers, was a Marxist think-tank that originated among a group of German intellectuals in the 1920s. The school initially consisted of dissident Marxists, who were concerned that some of the prophecies of Karl Marx regarding the eventual collapse of capitalism and the triumph of a classless socialist proletariat were not coming to pass. These intellectuals, repelled by the Leninist call to violent revolution, sought other pathways to change society. The primary goal of the Frankfurt School was to translate Marxism into cultural terms, and so provide the ideas for a new political theory of revolution based on culture, and on the harnessing of new oppressed groups.

Christianity that supported segregation in the South and apartheid in South Africa?'[4]

Tim Keller explains that when he found a 'band of brothers', a group of 'Christians who had a concern for justice in the world… grounded in the nature of God', things began to change for him.[5] Increasingly, he 'became interested in shaping and initiating new Christian communities', and thus he 'entered [the ministry] just a few years after college'.[6] Living out the neo-Marxist ideology of the Frankfurt School within the church became the goal of his life.

In *The Reason for God*, he looks forward to his followers being the 'vanguard of some major new religious, social and political arrangements'.[7] He claims, 'The purpose of Jesus' coming is to put the whole world aright, to renew and restore the creation…not just to bring personal forgiveness and peace, but also justice and shalom.'[8] This statement has a certain amount in common with the thinking of liberation theology, for 'in liberation theology, the Gospel is not a message about saving individuals out of the world, but rather a message of saving the world.'[9]

Tim Keller says that, 'the world and our hearts are broken. Jesus' life, death and resurrection was an infinitely costly rescue operation to restore justice to the oppressed and marginalized, physical wholeness to the diseased and dying, community to the isolated and lonely and spiritual joy and connection to those alienated from God.'[10] He explains that Jesus 'offers his lifeblood in order to honor moral justice and merciful love so that some day he can destroy all evil without destroying us'.[11] He also claims that, 'when Jesus suffered with us he was identifying with the oppressed of the world, not with their oppressors.'[12]

Some Bible-believing Christians may over-generously read into these sentiments an evangelical message, but Tim Keller's goal is to a great extent incongruous with, even antagonistic to, the purpose of the Gospel revealed in God's Word. He boldly declares: 'Jesus identified with the oppressed.'[13] In like manner, liberation theology claims that 'the God revealed in the biblical tradition in general and in Jesus Christ in particular, wills the liberation of the oppressed and is active in the world towards that end.'[14]

What Tim Keller claims as his 'new way of thinking about the Bible' is essentially the old liberation theology of the Latin American Roman Catholics. Jesuit priest, Juan Luis Segundo, one of the most important figures in the liberation theology movement, explains: 'God him/herself through Christ assumes and participates with us in the historical process of humanization and liberation, for this is the plan of God for humankind.'[15] Like them, on the social issue Tim Keller swerves from the central message of Scripture that this is a doomed world that cannot be restored, except by the coming of Christ and end-time events.

In line with liberation theology, Keller claims that, 'the work of the Spirit of God is not only to save souls but also to care [for] and cultivate the face of the earth, the material world.'[16] Of the many works of the Holy Spirit revealed in Scripture, caring for and cultivating the material world for its restoration and purity is not one. This is an invention of deviant thinkers adopted by Tim Keller to produce his 'new way of thinking about the Bible'. These heterodox interpretations are used by Tim Keller to support his insistence that the church is called to bring about societal change. It is a thesis that fits with the spirit of the age, rather than the work of the Spirit of God.

Tim Keller's social justice

In his book *Generous Justice* (2010), Keller builds upon the ideological foundation established in *The Reason for God*, revealing in more detail what he means by 'social justice'. In so doing, he confirms that his understanding of the problem of poverty is exactly that of the Frankfurt School of Marxism. Tim Keller begins *Generous Justice* by reminding us that 'the God of the Bible stood out from the gods of all other religions as a God on the side of the powerless, and of justice for the poor.'[17] He then mentions that Latin American theologian Gustavo Gutierrez, in his book *A Theology of Liberation* (1973),[18] speaks of God's 'preferential option for the poor'.[19] But he does not tell his readers that Gutierrez was a Dominican priest, widely accepted as the founder of liberation theology.

In Tim Keller we see a Christian utopian thinker who presents another version of the revised social gospel outlined in the 1970s by Ronald Sider in the book *Rich Christians in an Age of Hunger*, which raised the question: Is God a Marxist?

Generous Justice presents a seriously distorted understanding of the Gospel, with a Christianised but essentially Marxist view of the problem of man (victimisation of the proletariat by capitalist bour-geoisie) and its solution (restoration of rights and redistribution of wealth achieved by non-violent socio-political action). Tim Keller, of course, uses Christian language and no doubt sincerely, but his message is heavily weighted by the Frankfurt School ideology that first fascinated him as a college student. Nowhere in *Generous Justice* is the reader told that the overtowering priority of the church and its true mission is to 'teach all nations, baptizing them in the name of the Father, and of the Son, and of the Holy Ghost' *(Matthew 28.19).*

The problem of man, in Tim Keller's thinking, is not *just* rebel-lion against a holy God; it is social injustice *also*. The solution for man is not *just* the individual's faith alone in Christ alone, it is social justice. Further, Tim Keller assures his readers that they can bring about the desired social reformation, which Scripture says only God can do through the events at the return of Christ. This is an attrac-tive message to people who would not respond to an unadorned call to repentance, but may come to Christ to participate in the (humanly) appealing objective of a reformed earthly society. The worldly heart will respond to an appeal to participate in a heroic mission to socially restore the world. This is a theology that also appeals to many Anglican people in the UK, meshing with their longing for an inspiring social purpose. When combined with the love of worldly entertainment and expression (as it is in Tim Keller's group of churches), it has a strong appeal to the natural mind. New Calvinists are generally astute at utilising human appeal.

Tim Keller's view of salvation

In 2006, at an Entrepreneur's Forum sponsored by Redeemer Church, Tim Keller expressed his disenchantment with conservative Christians, saying, 'Conservative churches say "this world is not our home – it's gonna burn up eventually and what really matters is saving souls...so evangelism and discipleship and saving souls are what is important". And we [that is, Redeemer Church] try to say that it's the other way around almost. That the purpose of salvation is to renew creation. That this world is a good in itself.'[20]

In *The Reason for God*, Tim Keller elaborates further on social restoration: 'Christianity is not only about getting one's individual sins forgiven so we can go to Heaven. That is an important means of God's salvation, but not the final end or purpose of it.' As we saw above, Tim Keller believes that the ultimate purpose of redemption is to put the whole world right. 'In short, the Christian life means not only building up the Christian community through encouraging people to faith in Christ, but building up the human community through deeds of justice and service. Christians, then, are the true revolutionaries who work for justice and truth...'[21] So Keller's supreme 'salvation' is about saving the world from injustice and oppression, while the Gospel of salvation from sin is a means to that end.

Muting of clear witness

Keller expresses his dislike for those whom he labels Christian fanatics. He says that the biggest deterrent to Christianity for the average person is the shadow of fanaticism. He writes, 'Many non-believers have friends or relatives who have become "born again" and seem to have gone off the deep end. They soon begin to express loudly their disapproval of various groups and sectors of our society – especially movies and television, the Democratic Party, homosexuals, evolutionists…When arguing for the truth of their faith they often appear intolerant and self-righteous. This is what many people would call fanaticism.'[22] It is clear that he is not referring to a small number of unwise, negatively-minded believers, but to all those who are direct in their manner of witness, because he calls them the 'biggest deterrent' to Christianity.

Keller argues that these born-again Christians are 'overbearing, self-righteous, opinionated, insensitive and harsh'. He appears to desire a more low-key, non-judgemental approach to evangelism, that does not risk offending – the very same policy of New Evangelicalism. Such an approach usually stresses apologetic arguments, and the positive earthly benefits of religion rather than salvation from sin.

Confusion over eternal punishment

In August 2011, Keller was invited by the Veritas Forum, a gathering of university academics and students in the USA, to deal with issues raised in *The Reason for God*. Interviewed by NBC journalist Martin Bashir, Keller presented his intellectual arguments for believing in God. The interview is online, and has been visited by many thousands of people.[23] Keller is asked whether Jesus Christ is the only way to God.

Bashir: 'I'm talking about the millions of Muslims, Sikhs and Jews who have heard about Jesus. Where does your thesis leave them?'

Keller: 'If Jesus is who he says he is, then, long term, they don't have God. If on the other hand…all I can always say about this is, God gives me, even as a minister with the Scripture, information on a need-to-know basis…If right now, a person doesn't have him, he or she needs to get him. If they die, and they don't have Jesus Christ, I don't know…I certainly know that God is wiser than me, more merciful than me, and I do know that, when I finally find out how

God is dealing with every individual soul, I won't have any questions about it…'

Pressed by Bashir on what happens to people of other religions, Tim Keller responds: 'People in other religions, unless they find Christ, I don't know any other way; but I also get information on a need-to-know basis, so if there's some *trapdoor*, or something like that, I haven't been told about it.'

Tim Keller says to be a Christian means that your soul has to 'get Jesus'. And he makes the remarkable statement, before a large audience, that God may just possibly have a *trapdoor* for unbelievers that he has not told us about. Keller is surmising that God may actually have an unrevealed way to Heaven for those who do not repent and place their faith in Christ. But Keller's *trapdoor* possibility is unbiblical and deeply heretical, for it implies, contrary to Scripture, that belief in Christ is not the only way of salvation for rational adults.

And the final shock – Tim Keller says that he does not know what happens to unbelievers who die without Christ. He says: 'If they die and they don't have Jesus Christ, I don't know…' But surely a theologian of his standing must know what Scripture says about those who die without Christ: 'He that believeth on the Son hath everlasting life: and he that believeth not the Son shall not see life; but the wrath of God abideth on him' *(John 3.36)*. So why does Tim Keller not refer to Scripture in answer to Martin Bashir's question? Does he find it embarrassing to hold to the Truth? Does not the slick avoidance of the convicting elements of the Gospel lead inevitably to the difficulty in which Tim Keller found himself in the interview?

Affinity with Rome

In *The Reason for God*, Tim Keller seeks support for his belief in theistic evolution by looking to the Church of Rome. He writes: 'For example, the Catholic Church, the largest church in the world, has made official pronouncements supporting evolution as being compatible with Christian belief.'[24] He appears to concede recognition to Rome, as a valid church, and the largest such in the world, to encourage Christian acceptance of evolution.

Tim Keller provides a definition of Christianity that includes all Orthodox, Roman Catholic and Protestant Christians who affirm the traditional creeds of the faith, such as the Apostles' Creed. He writes: 'What is Christianity? For our purposes, I'll define Christianity as the body of believers who assent to these great ecumenical creeds... I am making a case in this book for the truth of Christianity in general – not for one particular strand of it.'[25]

This statement shows that he makes no great distinction between the Protestant faith and Roman Catholicism, as he speaks of the whole church. Roman Catholicism is recognised as a valid 'strand' of Christianity, Protestantism being, presumably, a smaller 'strand', and evangelicalism an even smaller one. He does not appear to uphold the exclusive efficacy and legitimacy of the Gospel understood in an evangelical way.

Catholic authors and mysticism embraced

Tim Keller writes in *The Reason for God* that he could show the way of God's grace 'in a hundred famous spiritual biographies, such as those of St Paul, Augustine, Martin Luther, John Wesley'. But he has a favourite. He says, 'My favourite example of the trauma of grace is the one depicted by Flannery O'Connor in her short story "Revelation".'[26] He then spends two pages summarising O'Connor's short story, before concluding: 'What a radical idea! The "freaks and lunatics" going to Heaven before the morally upright tribe?'[27] Tim Keller makes other approving references to the writings of Mary Flannery O'Connor.

The *New World Encyclopedia* describes O'Connor as a life-long Roman Catholic, whose writing was deeply influenced by sacramental things. 'She wrote ironic, subtly allegorical fiction about deceptively backward Southern characters, usually fundamentalist Protestants, who undergo transformations of character that, in

O'Connor's view, brought them closer to the Catholic mind...'[28] The fact that Tim Keller chose to use O'Connor's writing to illustrate the meaning of grace tells us much about his real views, and how much broader they are than the reformed Confessions to which he subscribes. From the vast ocean of reformed literature which explains that salvation is by grace alone, through faith alone, in Christ alone, he chose to use a Catholic novelist, who undermines the reformed faith through her caricatures of 'fundamentalist' Protestant Christians.

Tim Keller quotes Catholic celebrities Malcolm Muggeridge, G. K. Chesterton and J. R. Tolkien in support of his theological and philosophical arguments. In his interview with *First Things*, America's premier Roman Catholic journal, he says: 'I don't want to defend just one kind of Christianity. I think I want to defend the Apostles' Creed.'[29] He wants non-believers to accept the Apostles' Creed, and then work out where they want to go. In this interview Keller is clear that his intention is to defend what he calls the 'whole Faith', and that includes defending the Church of Rome. We repeat, he is by no means the representative of an exclusively evangelical view of salvation.

The fruit of Tim Keller's accommodation of the Church of Rome is the acceptance and promotion of Catholic mystical practices in the church he pastors, Redeemer Church. In 2009, the church ran a series of talks to teach the congregation how to practise 'The Way of the Monk', a method of prayer and worship that is grounded in Catholic mysticism.[30] Tim Keller's addresses on the topic of Catholic mysticism show his outspoken acceptance of 16th-century Catholic mystics. He accepts their salvation, credits them with deep spirituality, and enthusiastically endorses their mystical contemplation techniques.

The Redeemer Church website explains the Catholic meditation technique of *Lectio Divina*, a Benedictine method of Bible reading involving mystical self-projection into the divine presence. The website also provides advice on, of all things, the *Spiritual Exercises* of Ignatius Loyola, founder of the Jesuits. An article on the website, entitled 'Meditation: Not So Mysterious', gives this advice: 'Loyola's methods, recorded in his book *Spiritual Exercises*, have been used for hundreds of years. He urged people to enter into Scripture with all five senses: sight, hearing, taste, touch, and smell.'[31]

One of the Redeemer flock was so disturbed by what was happening that she wrote: 'I had to finally leave Redeemer because I learned they are holding classes on how to pray by way of *Lectio Divina*, contemplative prayer/meditation, and even how to create "your own private monastery" (class was called The Way of the Monk). This most definitely does not sit well with me and I wrote a letter to the Pastors and Elders of the church about my concerns a couple of months ago but have not yet received a response.'[32]

Tim Keller's theistic evolution

Tim Keller is a firm believer in what he calls 'progressive evolution'. In *The Reason for God*, he seeks to help people overcome their doubts by persuading them of the 'truth' of theistic evolution, a theory that allows Christians to claim that they believe in both creation and evolution.

The science of evolution is regarded as being beyond question, and the Bible is so interpreted to conform to the 'truth' of science. Tim Keller does this by asserting that the first chapter of *Genesis* is a poem, and therefore cannot be taken literally.[33] He writes: 'I think *Genesis 1* has the earmarks of poetry and is therefore a "song" about the wonder and meaning of God's creation...For the record I think God guided some kind of process of natural selection, and yet I reject the concept of evolution as All-encompassing Theory.'[34]

Asked in a broadcast interview to clarify obvious difficulties in theistic evolution, Tim Keller responds: 'How could there have been death before Adam and Eve fell? The answer is, I don't know. But all I know is, didn't animals eat bugs? Didn't bugs eat plants? There must have been death. In other words, when you realize, "Oh wait, this is really complicated…"'[35]

Keller recognised that his account of theistic evolution was confused, saying that he prefers the 'messy' approach. But this approach – as he tries to explain it – appears to be without logic and coherence, and contradictory.

Contextualising the Gospel

Tim Keller stresses the importance of making the Gospel culturally sensitive. He asserts that man's resistance to the Gospel is inherently cultural, an unbiblical and anti-calvinistic view increasingly taken up by New Calvinists. Therefore, he says, the Gospel must 'be presented in connection with baseline cultural narratives – Jesus must be the answer to the questions the culture is asking. Don't forget – every Gospel presentation presents Jesus as the answer to some set of human-cultural questions…every Gospel presentation has to be culturally incarnated, it must assume some over-riding cultural concern…Christianity must be presented as answers to the main questions and aspirations of our culture.'[36]

In presenting the Gospel, says Keller, we must answer the question: What puts the world right? We must also explain how we can be part of putting the world right. Not only do these views reflect Tim Keller's claim that 'the primary purpose of salvation is – cultural renewal – to make this world a better place',[37] but they also show his practical sidelining of the reformed view he professes of man's wilful, sinful alienation from God – the only sound basis for authentic evangelism.

Conclusion

Tim Keller is a major force in New Calvinism. His views are widely propagated through The Gospel Coalition, the Redeemer Network, the Proclamation Trust in the UK, and conferences around the world. While he has a reputation for being a sound Protestant

Christian leader, the reality is that he is far from the principles of the reformed faith in many ways. He employs a pseudo-intellectual, philosophical approach to propagate Christian teaching. He extends the great commission to include the unauthorised task of global social restoration. He extends the definition of the church to include those who do not subscribe to the exclusive, soul-saving efficacy of the Gospel, evangelically understood. He promotes the doctrine of theistic evolution. He seeks to contextualise the Gospel to make it culturally acceptable, meaning, in practical terms, that worldly, entertainment-based evangelism and worship is acceptable. He is an archetypical New Calvinist, who has in practice moved far from the beliefs and practices of the Reformation.

3
John Piper and Theological Flexibility

W E NOW FOCUS on the influence on the New Calvinism of John Piper, well known as a best-selling author, conference speaker, and founder of *Desiring God Ministries*. An eloquent preacher and reformed theologian, he stands at the very centre of the movement. His intense personality and forceful, persuasive preaching style has made him extremely acceptable to young evangelical Christians in particular. An avowed Calvinist, his *Desiring God* website affirms: 'We begin as Bible-believing Christians who want to put the Bible above all systems of thought. But over the years we have deepened in our conviction that calvinistic teachings on the five points are biblical and therefore true.'[1]

John Piper first sensed God's call to enter the ministry while a student at Wheaton College, Chicago. He went on to earn degrees from Fuller Theological Seminary and the University of Munich, Germany (D.Theol). For six years he taught Biblical Studies at Bethel

College in St Paul, Minnesota, and in 1980 accepted the call to serve as pastor at Bethlehem Baptist Church in Minneapolis, Minnesota, where he ministered until 2013. He is the author of more than 30 books, including: *The Pleasures of God: Meditations on God's Delight in Being God* (1991), *The Hidden Smile of God* (2001), *Don't Waste Your Life* (2003), *What Jesus Demands from the World* (2006), and of course, the very best-selling *Desiring God: Meditations of a Christian Hedonist*, first published in 1986, and frequently reprinted.

In *Desiring God* John Piper aims to help readers embark on a different and joyful experience of their faith. The book has been called a twentieth-century classic that changes lives. Some reviews declare that, next to the Bible, *Desiring God* is the most life-changing book they have ever read. Such is the attraction of the term 'desiring God', that John Piper has successfully developed a specialised ministry that promotes his vision of so-called 'Christian hedonism'.

John Piper is highly sought after as a conference speaker. He usually gives the keynote address at the annual *Passion Conference*, already referred to, attended by many thousands of young people. His annual *Desiring God* conference in the USA attracts speakers from across the broader evangelical theological spectrum. In 2007, he spoke at the inaugural meeting of The Gospel Coalition, of which he is a council member. Despite his immense popularity, however, there is much in John Piper's ministry that encourages seriously mistaken trends in New Calvinism, and swerves from the traditional application to life of the calvinistic doctrines which he strongly upholds. This is very confusing for people new to the doctrines of grace, who have appreciated John Piper's books and sermons.

Desiring God

John Piper became famous in the evangelical world through the publication of *Desiring God*. This presents his 'Christian hedonism' philosophy of life based on the ideas of the Catholic philosopher Blaise Pascal, and C. S. Lewis. One of C. S. Lewis' sermons, 'The

Weight of Glory', had a really profound influence on him. 'I had never in my whole life heard any Christian, let alone a Christian of Lewis' stature, say that all of us not only seek (as Pascal said) but also ought to seek our own happiness.'[2, 3]

In *Desiring God*, John Piper recalls: 'All those years I had been trying to suppress my tremendous longing for happiness, so I could honestly praise God out of some "higher", less selfish motive. But now it started to dawn on me that this persistent and undeniable yearning for happiness was not to be suppressed, but to be glutted – on God.'[4] Piper's tremendous longing for happiness was to be nurtured and cultivated, and God was to be the source that satisfied his yearning. It has been pointed out that the index of *Desiring God* has twenty references to happiness and only one to holiness.

Here we should note that it is the unregenerate heart that sees happiness as the prime purpose of life. The apostle Paul prayed for better things for the Colossian saints desiring 'that ye might be filled with the knowledge of his will in all wisdom and spiritual under-standing; that ye might walk worthy of the Lord unto all pleasing' *(Colossians 1.9-10)*. Piper's flawed mentors inspired him to integrate their human aspirations with the Christian faith, and the result was Christian hedonism.

John Piper 'hears God'

John Piper's consequent emphasis on Christian hedonism produced a hopelessly over-simplified scheme for sanctification and also for discernment, leaving him unduly susceptible to religious sensationalism, including shafts of charismatic thinking, theatri-calism, and contemporary worship extremes.

John Piper's susceptibility to subjective influence is seen in his claim to have heard God speak, directly to him, from *Psalm 66.5-7*. He wrote on the *Desiring God* website – 'Let me tell you about a most wonderful experience I had early Monday morning, March 19, 2007, a little after six o'clock. God actually spoke to me. There is no doubt that it was God. I heard the words in my head just as clearly as when a memory of a conversation passes across your consciousness. The words were in English, but they had about them an absolutely self-authenticating ring of truth. I know beyond the shadow of a doubt that God still speaks today.' John Piper believes God said to him: 'Come and see what I have done.' God's voice also said: 'I keep watch over the nations – let not the rebellious exalt themselves.' He interpreted his ecstatic experience thus: 'He [God] may as well have taken me by the collar of my shirt, lifted me off the ground with one hand, and said, with an incomparable mixture of fierceness and love, "Never, never, never exalt yourself. Never rebel against me." '

It is a wonderful matter when a scripture comes home to the mind with great force, and one appreciates the sense and depth and wonder of the Word, but it is presumptuous to hear a voice, whether audible or as if it were audible, directed in a special visitation. It often suggests great spiritual pride, that a believer should feel so honoured. Yet charismatic subjectivism is increasingly approved of in the New Calvinism. The historic Protestant position affirms 'that the Word of God, spoken through apostles and prophets, and intended for the direction of his church, is now found only in sacred Scripture'.[5]

How sad it is if thousands of young Christians are not taught the safe principles of the Word, which alone can keep them from charismatic delusion.

John Piper and contemporary worship

At the centre of Piper's ministry is a deep commitment to contemporary, worldly worship and to the 'Christian' rap scene. He publicly demonstrated his support by inviting the popular rap artist Lecrae to perform during a morning service in Bethlehem Baptist Church when he was pastor. The artist received a standing ovation from an enthusiastic congregation.[6] So close is the relationship between John Piper and Lecrae that their respective organisations, *Desiring God* and Reach Records, have worked together to produce a 'holy' hip-hop DVD.

But perhaps nothing illustrates John Piper's promotion of the holy hip-hop scene more than his involvement with the annual *Passion Conference* organised by Louie Giglio. He was the keynote speaker at *Passion 2013*, held in Atlanta Dome, Georgia, which attracted an audience of sixty thousand young people from across the world. Yet it is not difficult for a Christian believer to discern that *Passion* worship is very different from the biblical under-standing of worship. Our Lord said: 'God is a Spirit: and they that worship him must worship him in spirit and in truth' *(John 4.24)*. *Passion* worship is based on a culture of rock music and psychedelic lighting that produces a spirit of revelry. Led by Christian rock artist Chris Tomlin and Christian rapper Lecrae, the young audience was worked into a state of ecstatic excitement. Into this toxic atmos-phere, John Piper, emerging theatrically through the darkness, took to the podium and preached to the massive crowd.[7]

Remarkably, he preached in the dark, except for a spotlight that focused on him. Why no light? Because the mystical, ecstatic atmos-phere of *Passion*, so carefully cultivated by the mix of darkness, psychedelic strobe lights, and relentless, overpoweringly loud beat music, would have been shattered if the youthful audience had been brought to its senses. *Passion* does not aim at that; it wants young people to be held captive under the intoxicating spell of the clubbing atmosphere.

A faithful Bible preacher, preaching the Gospel of Truth, ought surely to require that the lights be turned on in order that the congregation could refer to the biblical text, and listen in the light of normal rationality. But John Piper was perfectly happy to preach in surrounding darkness, conforming to the ethos and spirit of the *Passion Conference* which is all about sensational, mood-managing worldly music and the cultivation of a spirit of revelry. He lends his vast reputation to influence young people into approving manipulative communication and compromise with the world. By this he makes the depraved *Passion* culture acceptable to reformed teachers and churches.

The exploitation and approval of charismatic worship and theatricalism is far out of accord with reformed principles and has been given a seemingly irreversible impetus by the teaching of John Piper and his fellow New Calvinists.

John Piper and discernment

To the great surprise of many, in 2010 John Piper invited Rick Warren, author of *The Purpose Driven Life* and pastor of Saddleback Church of Southern California, to address the *Desiring God* national conference. Explaining his reason for the invitation, Piper said: 'I do think he is deeply theological, he's a brilliant man...So I don't think he's emergent – at root I think he is theological and doctrinal and sound.'[8]

Yet Rick Warren is well known as an 'easy-believism' exponent, of thoroughly ecumenical (even multi-faith) outlook, and far from a sound calvinistic conviction.

In 2011 John Piper sat for an interview with Rick Warren in the studios of Saddleback Church to discuss the doctrinal issues surrounding *The Purpose Driven Life*. Up until then, most reformed preachers regarded it as being so extreme in its seeker-sensitive Arminianism as to constitute a false gospel. Nevertheless, John Piper asserted that he had no problem with the book, which he said had been much maligned by most reformed theologians. He went as far as to say, 'Frankly, I'm appalled at the kinds of slander that have been brought against this book.'[9]

John Piper used his weight and acceptance as a leader among reformed believers to persuade them that Rick Warren has been misinterpreted and misunderstood, and was in fact 'one of us'. So close is the fellowship that developed between the two men that a regional *Desiring God* conference was held in Rick Warren's Saddleback Church in California in April 2011.[10]

John Piper undoubtedly stands at the very centre of the New Calvinism, but his readiness to embrace as authentic Calvinism an extreme example of easy-believism and pragmatic gimmickry shows him to be remarkably unreliable as a guide. His rejection of the doctrine that signs and revelatory gifts have ceased has also made him an unsound guide in one of the most dangerous departures from conservative faith, and left him indifferent and open to charismatic practices. His philosophy of Christian hedonism is deeply flawed, providing a novel and inadequate motive for striving in holiness to the people of God. Furthermore, John Piper's promotion of contemporary worship even in its very worst manifestations, such as the holy hip-hop movement, has encouraged the widening collapse into irreverent, worldly worship, and is misleading thousands of young people into worldly and deeply damaging personal leisure music. His toleration of inconsistent conduct seen in his support of Mark Driscoll and prominent rappers does nothing to promote confidence in his discernment.

When a measure of doctrinal soundness is accompanied by such serious mistakes, the damage to God's people is far greater than where the erring person is altogether unsound in doctrine. If pastors and churches are influenced to adopt the same looseness in implementing conservative convictions there will be untold harm to Gospel work, and vulnerable believers will be plunged into tragic worldliness. Equally, unbelievers will be called to respond to a Christ who embraces the world, a message which will not lead them to true conversion. The tragedy of all this compels us to sound this warning.

4
Mark Driscoll
Proponent of 'Cultural Relevance'

MARK DRISCOLL, senior pastor of Mars Hill Church in Seattle, and co-founder of the church planting *Acts 29 Network*, is easily one of the most influential men in the New Calvinism. He has the reputation of being the world's most downloaded and quoted pastor. In 2012 Mars Hill Church had around 14,000 attendees at its fourteen locations in Seattle. The *Acts 29 Network* has planted over 400 churches, and is active in the UK and thirteen other nations. Mark Driscoll has also founded *The Resurgence*, a theological cooperative that produces teaching resources.

Mark Driscoll is so popular that he is invited to talk at many Christian conferences in the USA and across the world. In May 2011, he was invited by evangelical Christians in the UK to preach before 4,000 men at the *London Men's Convention* in the Royal Albert Hall.

Mark Driscoll claims to be firmly in the calvinistic camp. He affirms that John Calvin is one of the greatest teachers in the history of the Church. He said: 'I really appreciate his work, and I named my middle son Calvin Martin, after John Calvin and Martin Luther. This tells you what team I'm on.'[1]

Mark Driscoll praises New Calvinism and names four ways in which he thinks it is better than traditional Calvinism. First, he feels Old Calvinism was fundamental and separated from culture, whereas New Calvinism is missional and seeks to create and redeem culture. Second, he maintains that Old Calvinism fled from the cities, while New Calvinism is flooding into cities. Third, Old Calvinism was cessationistic and fearful (or so he thinks) of the presence of the Holy Spirit. New Calvinism is continuationist and joyful in the presence and power of the Holy Spirit. Fourth, Old Calvinism was fearful and suspicious of other Christians and burned bridges, whereas New Calvinism loves all Christians and builds bridges between them. Putting aside the inaccuracies, these views leave no doubt about his hostility to the biblical duty of separation from worldliness, and his charismatic inclinations.

Despite his popularity in the evangelical world, Mark Driscoll's ministry has proved highly controversial because of his unconventional methods, which he describes as 'theologically conservative and culturally liberal'. Here are the controversial characteristics of his ministry:–

1. Brings licentiousness into the church

From the beginning of his ministry, Mark Driscoll has sought to gain attention by using sexually provocative language, and his writing is full of it. He built his fame, in large part, by his early preaching and teaching about sex, and use of smutty language. In his book, *Confessions of a Reformission Rev* (2006), he explains his technique for achieving church growth. He assumed that young people were all interested in sex, and so he preached through the *Song of Solomon*, which he interpreted as a sex manual.

Although he preaches that sex is for marriage, his manner of referring to sexual matters is objectionably sensuous and flippant. In 2007, Mark Driscoll preached in two churches in Scotland. He offered the congregation a choice of three sermons. Amid cheers and laughter, they chose sex in the *Song of Solomon*. The sermon, entitled 'Sex, a study of the Good Bits from *Song of Solomon*', focused on unnatural sexual acts performed by the wife on her husband. His message for a wife was this: 'If you think you're being dirty, he's pretty happy.' Mark Driscoll's teaching was so explicit that it caused outrage. John MacArthur referred to the sermon as soft porn.

2. Dishonours marriage

Mark Driscoll has carefully cultivated the idea that he teaches sex is only for marriage, and that he is against fornication, homo-sexuality and pornography. Yet a careful examination of what he has actually been teaching for over two decades shows a very disturbing picture. His book, *Real Marriage,* published January 2012, is significant for it gives details of what he teaches about sex in marriage. In a chapter entitled, 'Can We—?' Mark Driscoll asserts that a catalogue of unnatural sexual acts are biblically permissible in marriage. He writes: 'Legally and biblically anal sex is permissible for a married couple as Scripture does not forbid it.' He presents an argument claiming to show that 'anal sex within marriage is not sodomy, is not inherently sinful, and is permissible.'[2] He endorses sexual role-play in marriage: 'Role playing is when one or both spouses assume roles to act out in character as part of their flirta-tion and lovemaking…Some couples with good imaginations find it fun.'[3] He says that there 'are many reasons cosmetic surgery [breast augmentation] may be beneficial. It can make us more attractive to our spouse. And if our appearance is improved, we feel more comfortable being seen naked by our spouse, which can increase our freedom in lovemaking.'[4] He goes on to discuss a range of other deviant sexual acts which he says are biblically permissible in marriage, including the use of sex toys, oral sex, sexual medication, and cyber sex.

Pastor Tim Challies of Grace Fellowship Church in Toronto comments: 'As a husband I would not want my wife to read some of what this chapter contains. This is not prudishness but protection.' [5]

Denny Burk, Associate Professor of Biblical Studies at Boyce College, writes: 'Among the activities that the authors deem permissible within this taxonomy are masturbation, felatio/cunnilingus, sodomy (on both spouses), menstrual sex, role-playing, sex toys, birth control, cosmetic surgery, cybersex, and sexual medication... Yet the Driscolls give explicit instructions to wives about how they might sodomize their husbands in a pleasurable way (p. 188). Yet where in the Bible is such an activity ever commended?'[6]

Some of what Mark Driscoll says is true, such as sex is meant for marriage and fornication is wrong, but this does not give him the authority to assert that unnatural sexual acts are permissible in marriage. He is encouraging Christians to ignore the long-held Christian consensus, and to adopt things that should never even be mentioned among God's people.

Scripture emphasises the purity of the marriage union. 'Marriage is honourable in all, and the bed undefiled: but whoremongers and adulterers God will judge' *(Hebrews 13.4)*. The marriage bed, a euphemistic phrase for the sexual relationship between husband and wife, is to be undefiled and clean. The purity of the marriage union is to be honoured and preserved. Scripture uses euphemistic language for the intimacy of the marital union, thereby teaching us that we should think and speak about the physical side of the marriage union with great care and delicacy. This is an important principle in protecting marriage, for marriage is honoured and the bed undefiled when we combine absolute purity of mind with firmly guarded speech. Mark Driscoll's deviant, unnatural, shameful sexual acts dishonour marriage, and his explicit, raw, undignified sexual language degrades and defiles the marriage bed.

3. Treads a dangerous path on pornography

Turning to Driscoll's teaching on pornography, we note that in his book *Radical Reformission* (2004), as part of what he calls a cultural immersion project, he suggests that men should read *Cosmo Girl* magazine and listen to salacious sex-talk radio programmes. Furthermore, in *Real Marriage* Driscoll, though saying he condemns it, discusses the porn industry in detail.

Heath Lambert, assistant Professor of Pastoral Theology at Boyce College, Louisville, Kentucky, in a review of *Real Marriage*, comments: 'make no mistake: men and women will be introduced to pornography because of this book…The Driscolls introduce their readers to the titles of pornographic books, magazines, and videos; they provide technical names for specific kinds of pornographic films; they list the names of celebrities who have starred in pornography; they even provide web addresses where readers can meet people for sex. As I look back on that sentence I am overwhelmed that a Christian minister could be so irresponsible.' [7]

Using his supposed gift of discernment, Mark Driscoll claims in one of his teaching sessions (recorded on YouTube), that God showed him a vision of a woman in his congregation engaging in an adulterous act in a cheap hotel room. His vision of the sex act was so explicit, because the lights were left on, that he claims to have seen the colour of the bedspread, and even the colour of the man's eyes and his blond hair. Mark Driscoll said to the woman, whom he was accusing of adultery in the presence of her husband, that: 'And deep down in your heart…you desired him because secretly he is the fantasy body type.' [8] What thoughts are in the mind of a pastor who claims to have visions of adulterous sex?

The Mars Hill Church website provides hyperlinks to two pornographic websites, one of which deals with sex toys and the other is entitled 'Christian Nymph'. Dr Judith Reisman (an expert on the flawed research and writings of Alfred Kinsey), having viewed Mark

Driscoll's recommended websites said: 'Well, this is, at best, tragic. I don't know if it is worse to think that these are phony church sites put out by pornographers or that they are real church sites put out by pornified churches. Words cannot describe the ignorance, arrogance and flagrant homoeroticism of these sites.' These websites, of course, can be freely viewed by unmarried young people in Mars Hill Church and the wider world.

4. Use of coarse language and worldly presentation

In his ministry Driscoll has frequently used coarse language. Even in sermons his language has been lewd and vulgar. He became so well known for using profane language that in the book *Blue Like Jazz*,[9] Donald Miller, popular author and icon of the Emerging Church movement, nicknamed him 'Mark the Cussing Pastor'.[10] In recent years he has somewhat modified his language.

Another feature of Driscoll's ministry is his casual dress in the pulpit. When preaching in Mars Hill Church he often wears jeans with provocative T-shirts. Examples include T-shirts with the following slogans: 'Body piercing saved my life'; 'Jesus is my homeboy'; 'Mary is my homegirl'. He has worn those bearing an image of Drag Queen Jesus, with the caption, 'Jesus watches you download porn'. Other T-shirts include images of Mickey Mouse, skull and cross bones, and Jesus as a DJ.[11]

5. The mocking of Scripture

Mark Driscoll often makes light of Scripture and makes fun of biblical characters. Gideon, a Judge of Israel and the Lord's warrior, commended as a hero of the faith in *Hebrews 11.32-33*, is labelled by him a complete coward. John the Baptist is a freak. In a sermon on humour in the Bible, he says the book of *Genesis* is where all things begin, including good comedy. He says: 'I mean the whole book is a redneck, hillbilly saga, par excellence. It's like all of *Genesis* takes place in a trailer park...the whole book is filled with redneck comedy…That's how I see it. It's kind of funny that after God kills everyone, the one "righteous" guy passes out naked in his tent.'[12]

Mark Driscoll's book, *Vintage Jesus* (2007), co-authored with theologian Dr Gerry Breshears, while containing some doctrinal truth, also contains much which is crude and offensive. It is widely available in Christian bookshops in the USA and UK. Many church bookstalls promote this book, and thousands of young people have read it. It is no example to them of how believers should think and speak of God's Book.

Here are a few quotations from *Vintage Jesus*[13]: 'In the first chapter of *Mark*, Jesus starts off by yelling at complete strangers to repent of their sin…In the second chapter, Jesus picks a fight with some well-mannered religious types…

'In the third chapter, Jesus gets angry and also grieves, and apparently needs Praxil *[an anti-depressant]*…Then he ignores his own mom…In chapter 5, Jesus kills two thousand pigs, sending the animal rights activist blogosphere into a panic, and creating a bacon famine…In chapter 6, Jesus offends some people and apparently needs sensitivity training. In chapter 7, a few religious types have some questions for Jesus, and he cruelly calls them "hypocrites" and goes on a lengthy tirade about them…' He also claims, 'Jesus was actually a pretty fun guy because he got invited to a lot of parties…'[14] So his arrogant comedy goes on with provocative and inane comments about each chapter in *Mark's Gospel*. The picture he paints of the Lord Jesus Christ is frequently irreverent and blasphemous, flippant and mocking. He draws his conclusion: 'In summary, the Jesus of *Mark's Gospel* is not fitting for old ladies in hats and men in suits like those we see at church.'

Throughout his work Mark Driscoll reveals a strong dislike for those he calls 'religious people', by which he means traditional Bible-believing churchgoers; taking every opportunity to condemn them as 'fundamentalists…prone to legalism, moralism, and a general lack of love, grace or patience'. Yet for all this *Vintage Jesus* has been widely praised by many prominent evangelical leaders. Professor of Christian Theology at Southern Baptist Theological Seminary, Bruce Ware, enthusiastically endorsed the book, saying, 'Vintage Jesus offers a fresh, engaging, and insightful discussion of some of the oldest and most crucial truths about Jesus Christ that constitute the very core of the Gospel itself. As I read, my heart leapt for joy, for the wonder and brilliance of the truths being developed...'[15]

Wayne Grudem, Professor of Theology and Biblical Studies at Phoenix Seminary, Arizona, was equally fulsome in his praise of Vintage Jesus: 'Mark Driscoll and Gerry Breshears combine profound understanding of modern culture with weighty Christian doctrine that is faithful to the Bible. It's written in such an interesting style that it's hard to put down. I strongly recommend it!'[16] Vintage Jesus has also been endorsed by John Piper, and the Desiring God organisation has promoted it.

6. Secular rock bands and the loudest rock music

Mark Driscoll's church-building methodology requires that Christians should engage with the culture of the day, irrespective of whether a style of behaviour or music was devised to promote sin. Worldly punk rock music forms a major part of his life and ministry. He has called hip-hop artist Jay-Z a genius, and referred to Christian rap artist Lecrae as a missionary of the 21st century. His love of hard rock music is a major force at Mars Hill Church. In Confessions of a Reformission Rev Driscoll says that he envisioned 'a large church that hosted concerts for non-Christian bands'.[17]

He writes in Radical Reformission: 'I was torn between buying the "secular" music that I enjoyed and the Christian music that I did not. After much prayer, I decided that God loved me and allowed my [Christian] music to be stolen so that I could buy back the old albums that I enjoyed. And so I did, and as pastor of a church filled with "secular" bands that hosts "secular" concerts, I have not had a regret since.'[18] John Piper described the music in Driscoll's church as the loudest he had ever heard. The employment of extreme rock in worship and evangelism is a policy employed by almost all the leading figures in New Calvinism.

7. Endorses supernatural visions

Mark Driscoll makes the alarming claim that he has a gift of discernment that allows him to see the sins of people in his congregation. In a seminar on counselling, he made the statement: 'Some people actually see things. This may be the gift of discernment. On occasions, I see things. I see things.' He claimed that he saw a person being sexually abused as a child. He said, 'It's like I got a TV right here. I'm seeing it…But some of you have this visual ability to see things.'

He went on to explain: 'It's the supernatural. It's the whole other realm. It's like the Matrix. You can take the blue pill, you take the red pill. You go into this whole other world. And that's the way it works…I see things too. I've seen women raped. I've seen children molested. I've seen people abused. I've seen people beaten. I've seen horrible things done.'[19]

Having rejected the cessation of sign and revelatory gifts, he swerves far from a biblical view of how the Spirit works through the Word, exposing himself and those who follow him to arrogant delusions. Conservative evangelicalism used to hold its adherents safely within sane and scriptural standards of conduct, but not in the New Calvinism.

8. Claims – 'Jesus loves tattoos'

Mark Driscoll's church supports tattoo artists in their work. The issue of tattoos is discussed on the 'Mars Hill Downtown Campus' under the headline: 'Jesus Loves Tattoos'. There is no objection made to Christian people being tattooed. In a sermon Mark Driscoll boldly asserted: 'You are free in Christ to be weird…Let me just say our position is this – tattoos are not a sin, right. Jesus Christ is going to have a tattoo – *Revelation* says on his second coming. It says that down his right leg will be written King of Kings and Lord of Lords, which will be really freakish for all the fundamentalists to see – Jesus all tattooed up. I can't wait for that day.'[20]

By promoting tattoos, Mark Driscoll encourages young people to make foolish decisions they will have to live with, and seriously undermines their sense of responsibility to Christ. Throughout history the tattoo has carried the mark of paganism, and for generations Christians have felt the emphatic command of the Old Testament was to be respected even in the present era – 'Ye shall not make any cuttings in your flesh for the dead, nor print any marks upon you: I am the Lord' *(Leviticus 19.28)*. Bible believers know that their body is the temple of the Holy Spirit, and for this reason the idea of having tattoos put on them after conversion is deeply repugnant to them. The New Calvinism of teachers like Mark Driscoll contemptuously dismisses godly traditions as they plant their now culturally liberal outlook on churches.

Is Mark Driscoll a false teacher?

Mark Driscoll presents himself as theologically conservative and culturally liberal. He claims that he has 'a Gospel of freedom'.[21] But his 'Gospel of freedom', as we have seen in this chapter, is one that is free from the rules and conduct of traditional biblical Christianity. So is he to be considered a false teacher? This is a question that confuses many.

We see a vast gulf between what Driscoll proclaims and the conduct that he promotes through his culturally liberal ministry. Those who support his ministry refer to sermons that they think are doctrinally correct. Those who reject his ministry point to the worldly speech, tone, tastes and conduct he projects. They ask – What is the value of elements of soundness when they are united with contradictory behaviour?

So again we ask, is Mark Driscoll to be regarded as a false teacher?

Our Lord gave the definitive test – 'Beware of false prophets, which come to you in sheep's clothing, but inwardly they are ravening wolves. *Ye shall know them by their fruits.* Do men gather grapes of thorns, or figs of thistles? Even so every good tree bringeth forth good fruit; but a corrupt tree bringeth forth evil fruit. A good tree cannot bring forth evil fruit, neither can a corrupt tree bring forth good fruit. Every tree that bringeth not forth good fruit is hewn down, and cast into the fire. *Wherefore by their fruits ye shall know them'* (*Matthew 7.15-20,* emphasis added).

We have seen above some of Mark Driscoll's conduct and *manner* of teaching, all doubtless communicating a standard of behaviour to his hearers:

1) Bringing licentiousness into the church.
2) Dishonouring marriage.
3) Treading a dangerous path on pornography.
4) Using coarse language and worldly presentation.
5) Mocking and making light of Scripture.
6) Revelling in and exploiting extreme worldly rock music.
7) Endorsing supernatural visions and gifts.
8) Promoting tattoos.

Mark Driscoll's popularity

For all this, Mark Driscoll is extremely popular among New Calvinists. He has received enormous support and encouragement from other leaders within the New Calvinism on both sides of the Atlantic. He is a regular speaker at large evangelical conferences worldwide.

Perhaps the greatest endorsement of Mark Driscoll's ministry has come from John Piper, who has twice invited Mark Driscoll to speak at the *Desiring God* conference. He has said that he loves Mark Driscoll's theology, and he is his friend. He has also indicated that he helps Driscoll as a father helps his son.

Significantly, Mark Driscoll has often preached at the annual

Gospel Coalition conference in the USA. In 2009, the title of Driscoll's sermon was 'Rightly Dividing the Word of Truth'. He started the sermon: 'I want to thank Dr Carson, whom I love and appreciate very much, and Dr Tim Keller for bringing us all together...what holds us together is theological conviction, and that's really what matters most...' In 2011 Driscoll preached on 'The Spirit-Filled Missional Ministry of Jesus', promoting his *Acts 29* vision of church-planting. The Gospel Coalition has wholly endorsed Mark Driscoll's ministry, and gives him every opportunity to promote his version of the Christian faith. Indeed, he has been so well accepted in The Gospel Coalition that at the 2011 national conference he was part of a panel discussion dealing with the issue of 'Training the Next Generation of Pastors and Other Christian Leaders'. The panel was chaired by Don Carson, with Mark Driscoll comfortably seated in the midst of some of the most significant names in New Calvinism.[22] In 2012 he resigned as a member of The Coalition Council, but his links remain.

We are bound to ask, how extreme does a preacher have to be, and how inconsistent does his behaviour have to become, before the ranks of New Calvinism cease to endorse, encourage and invite him? It is seemingly a movement lacking clear biblical standards of practice and conduct.

5
New Calvinism in the UK
The Proclamation Trust

WHILE THE TERM is seldom heard in the UK, the ideas and practices of New Calvinism have penetrated deeply into the UK evangelical camp. Three figureheads from the USA, namely Tim Keller, John Piper and Mark Driscoll, have become hugely influential among British evangelicals.

This chapter will show how the Proclamation Trust, an organisation of Christians mainly of Anglican persuasion, who aim to promote biblical preaching and calvinistic doctrine, are wholly committed to the compromises of New Calvinism. Founded in 1986 by St Helen's Church, Bishopsgate, London, the Proclamation Trust organises the annual Evangelical Ministry Assembly (EMA) and the Cornhill Training Course, which now trains around 90 students each year for various roles in Christian ministry.

The EMA attracts around a thousand participants listening to speakers from across the world. The Proclamation Trust also runs an extensive programme of residential conferences for ministers, theological students, women in ministry, lay preachers and ministers' wives. Their 'Project Timothy' also seeks to take Christian resources to developing countries.[1]

Theistic evolution

The Proclamation Trust, despite upholding 'the divine inspiration and infallibility of Holy Scripture', does not entirely stand in the reformed interpretative tradition. It is heavily influenced by the much weaker view now associated with New Calvinists which makes many concessions to liberal critics, and the 'cultural context' of Scripture. By way of example we may point to the promotion of theistic evolution. The Rev Vaughan Roberts of St Ebbe's Church, Oxford, and president of the Proclamation Trust, helps students to understand the first chapters of *Genesis* by referring them to Tim Keller's essay on progressive theistic evolution. The Proclamation Trust's sympathy with theistic evolution, based on the assertion that the first chapters of *Genesis* are poetic in style, and therefore not to be taken literally, is similar to the position of Tim Keller. The 'facts' of evolutionary science are placed on an equal footing with Scripture, as *Genesis* is interpreted through the lens of evolutionary theory. Many even question the historicity of Adam and Eve. We would be hard pressed to find a Cornhill student who is prepared to defend a six-day view of creation. Those who teach six-day creation are considered to be hard-line fundamentalists who are blind to the advances of science.

Here we should make the obvious point that theistic evolution has serious theological consequences for the Gospel. In many ways it can be seen as the original compromise, for it undermines the authority of Scripture by turning the creation element into poetic symbolism, which in turn casts doubt on the historicity of Adam and Eve, the reality of the Fall, and thus the plan and purpose of redemption.

Tim Keller at EMA

A feature of the Evangelical Ministry Assembly is its profound commitment to Tim Keller's view of the Gospel. Since 2000 Tim Keller has been a keynote speaker on four occasions, more often than any other overseas speaker. It appears that his seemingly intellectual and 'reasonable' approach has a special attraction for the Proclamation Trust. In 2011, Tim Keller addressed three EMA plenary sessions on 'Preaching that Connects', speaking on how preaching can be both contemporary in its application and rooted in orthodox Christianity. There is no doubt that the Proclamation Trust is deeply impressed with Tim Keller's presentation of the Christian message, and is providing a platform to promote it in the UK.

John Piper at EMA

John Piper has also been the keynote speaker at EMA on three occasions. In 2003, he gave three addresses on the 'Supremacy of God'. In 2006, he gave two addresses – 'Venturing in Ministry' and 'Enduring in Ministry'. In 2010, EMA revealed the fuzziness of its convictions with a conference that had a distinctly charismatic flavour. Piper spoke on 'Living by the Power of the Spirit' and 'Preaching in the Power of the Spirit'. Other speakers included Wayne Grudem (one of the main apologists for reuniting charismatic and conservative churches), John Coles (director of New Wine, the largest UK network of charismatic churches) and Terry Virgo (who founded Newfrontiers, another large network of charismatic churches).

Mark Driscoll

Mark Driscoll is so highly regarded among evangelical Anglican churches associated with the Proclamation Trust that he was invited to address the *London Men's Convention* in 2011. Mark Driscoll has also been involved in church-planting seminars in churches associated with the Proclamation Trust.

Contemporary worship

Like New Calvinists in the USA, most of the churches within the Proclamation Trust's sphere of influence are given over to the contemporary worship scene. Some have a music director, many have a worship band, and most sing contemporary songs which have emerged from the charismatic movement. The Proclamation Trust's director of ministry, Adrian Reynolds, in his article 'Pastor, lead the singing!',[2] gives this advice to worship leaders:

'When choosing modern songs, draw on recent songwriters who write content-rich songs: the Gettys, Stuart Townend [all charismatics], Steve and Vicki Cook [both are part of C. J. Mahaney's charismatic Sovereign Grace Church, USA], Bob Kauflin [director of the same organisation]...'[3] [Square brackets added.]

'Music Ministry'

'Music Ministry' is an organisation run by a collection of church music workers and pastors from a variety of churches around the UK closely associated with the Proclamation Trust. Music Ministry seeks to train, equip and serve local churches, encouraging them in their use of contemporary worship. The 2011 *London Music Ministry* conference was held in St Helen's Church, Bishopsgate, with Christopher Ash of the Cornhill training course as the main speaker. Andy Fenton, from Dundonald Co-Mission and leader of Music Ministry, spoke on the importance of combining biblically driven worship with what he called culturally sensitive music. He said that Music Ministry believes that biblically driven worship and culturally sensitive music are a necessity for each other. The problem, he thought, is that although music is huge in our culture, it is diminished in our churches.

Andy Fenton asserted that biblically driven worship is a feature

of traditional, orderly, dull, conservative churches, while culturally sensitive worship is rhythm driven by the percussion section of
the band. Some people don't understand the need for both aspects.
This, said Fenton, leaves young people with a terribly difficult deci-
sion. 'Do they go to the church with the music which resonates with
their hearts, and their minds, and their iPods, where it is "culturally sensitive", or do they go to the really good Bible-teaching church
where the music is pretty rubbish…Never, ever, have Bible-believing
churches been so out of touch musically with our culture.'

Fenton claims that charismatic churches grow because they have
fantastic music – they are culturally sensitive, for they play the type
of music that is on the people's iPods.[4] Fenton is using the term
'culturally sensitive' to make the music of the world appear acceptable to the church. But he entirely avoids the biblical concept of
worldliness, and the sin-promoting purpose and association of the
rock genre. He sees no application for the command – 'Love not
the world, neither the things that are in the world. If any man love
the world, the love of the Father is not in him. For all that is in the
world, the lust of the flesh, and the lust of the eyes, and the pride of
life, is not of the Father, but is of the world' *(1 John 2.15-16)*. Music
Ministry, which passionately promotes the contemporary music
scene, is teaching an unbiblical message that encourages Christians
to conform to the pattern of the world *(Romans 12.2)*.

Conclusion

The Proclamation Trust has become a major mouthpiece of the
New Calvinism in the UK. Without reservation, the Trust has ener-
getically promoted Tim Keller's version of the Gospel – a version
that believes that the purpose of Christ's coming is to put the world
right before his return; a version that holds to theistic evolution; a
version that surmises that God may have a *trapdoor* to Heaven for
people of other faiths; a version that regards ordinary born-again
believers who witness in clear terms as a great hindrance to souls;

a version that loves and promotes Catholic mystical devotions, and recognises Catholic spirituality; a version that teaches against separation from worldliness.

Accordingly the Trust's brand of Christianity is laced with love of the world, and given over to the contemporary worship scene, with bands, guitars and drums, with 'Christian rap and hip-hop' as well as the shallow songs of the charismatic movement. Casual and even immodest dress, informal worship and 'relaxed' church services, with a very generous sprinkling of jokes and applause, are all commonplace and 'cool', rather than reverence and awe at the holiness and majesty of God.

When Mark Driscoll was invited to the *London Men's Convention* in 2011 by a group of church leaders associated with the Proclamation Trust, why was no one willing to challenge his highly inconsistent aspects of conduct?

Whatever its founding intentions, we conclude that the Proclamation Trust is now a compromised organisation committed to the flawed teachings and practices of New Calvinism. It can only harm true Gospel work, and promote worldliness in the churches.

6
The Porterbrook Network and New Calvinism

IN THE PREVIOUS CHAPTER we saw how the Proclamation Trust has become the UK arm of New Calvinism. In this chapter we see how the Porterbrook Network, started by Dr Tim Chester and Pastor Steve Timmis, has become a UK arm of Mark Driscoll's church planting initiative. Tim Chester and Steve Timmis are the co-founders of an expanding group of small churches given the unusual name of *The Crowded House*, and co-authors of *Total Church*, a book which explains their alternative way of 'doing church'.[1] In 2013, both were also appointed to the faculty of Wales Evangelical School of Theology (WEST).

The Porterbrook Network is an organisation that describes itself as 'evangelical, reformed and missional, believing in the sovereign grace of God in salvation, the inerrancy of Scripture, substitutionary atonement and the missional identity of the church in every context.'[2] The Network is comprised of two branches – 'Porterbrook Learning' and the 'Porterbrook Seminary'.

The Porterbrook Learning programme, which began in 2007, aims to help 'ordinary Christians learn how to serve Jesus and his people better – whether they are church leaders, church planters, or simply Christians wanting to become more mission-focused'.[3] 'It is estimated that more than 1,200 Christians have participated in Porterbrook Learning since its launch, and a further 1,400 have studied individual modules in the context of their church or small group.'[4] According to the Porterbrook website, 'by God's grace, this is just the beginning!'

The Porterbrook Network desires to partner with like-minded organisations to aid in the development of Porterbrook Learning throughout the world. At the time of writing the main partners are *Acts 29 Network* in the USA and *Acts 29 Europe*. To really understand what the Porterbrook Network is all about, we need to know more about the two founders.

Tim Chester

Dr Tim Chester has a PhD on the relationship between mission and eschatology in the theology of Jürgen Moltmann. Moltmann is a liberal theologian, a universalist holding mystical views and approving much liberation theology. As we shall see later, he sees social liberation in the Christian mission, teaching that the second coming of Christ inspires Christians to strive for social change in the here and now.

Tim Chester describes *The Crowded House* as a network of missionary congregations, most of which meet in homes. 'We emphasise sharing our lives together rather than programmes and structures. "Ordinary life with Gospel intentionality" is one of our catch phrases.' He concedes that *The Crowded House* – 'is often described by other people as part of the emerging church movement. It is true that we have a different approach to church to that of most traditional churches. But we are also different from many in the emerging church movement. We are reformed and evangelical. Like conservatives we emphasise the centrality of the Gospel word. Like emerging church we emphasise the importance of the Gospel community.'[5] So Tim Chester feels that *The Crowded House* alternative way of 'doing church' is really a coming together of the emerging church and reformed evangelical Christianity.

The philosophy of *The Crowded House* is described in the book *Total Church*. Tim Chester is the author of many other books, including *Good News to the Poor: The Gospel through Social Involvement* (2004), in which he argues passionately that evangelism and social action are inseparable, as two arms of the church's mission. His books have proved popular with Mark Driscoll's Mars Hill Church in Seattle. In November 2010, the *Redeem Cities* conference held in Belfast, Northern Ireland, included as speakers Mark Driscoll and Tim Chester. The conference proclaimed how the church could transform culture, cities, and nations.[6]

Steve Timmis

Pastor Steve Timmis, co-founder of both *The Crowded House* and the Porterbrook Network, is also the director of the *Acts 29 Network* of church planters in Western Europe. Here we need to understand something about the *Acts 29 Network*, founded by Mark Driscoll. The mission of *Acts 29*, we are told, 'is to band together Christian, evangelical, missional and reformed churches, who, for the sake of Jesus and the Gospel, plant new churches and replant dead and dying churches across the United States and the world.'[7] The aim is to influence the shape of church planting culture through both theology and by contextualising the Gospel, which means expressing it through culturally relevant means (or worldly methods).

While Mark Driscoll resigned from the presidency of *Acts 29* in March 2012, he continues to play an active role in the leadership team.[8] Indeed, to explain its church planting philosophy, the website of *Acts 29* provides a hyperlink to Mark Driscoll's talk 'The Mission and Vision of *Acts 29*' (November 19, 2008).[9] Pastors who are part of the *Acts 29 Network* are provided with a list of Mark Driscoll's books, including titles such as *The Radical Reformission* (2004); *Confessions of a Reformission Rev: Hard Lessons from an Emerging Missional Church* (2006); *Vintage Jesus* (2008); *Vintage Church* (2008); *Porn-Again Christian* (2009) and *Doctrine: What Christians Should Believe* (2010).[10]

With the support of Mark Driscoll, *Total Church* was re-published in the USA by Crossways in 2008 as part of his own book series on church planting. The concepts of *Total Church* are entirely in tune with *Acts 29* thinking. Mark Driscoll wrote: 'I've been excited to see the growth of the *Acts 29* church planting movement into Great Britain and Western Europe under the direction of my friend Steve Timmis.'

Ethos and Policy of Porterbrook

The Porterbrook/*Crowded House* method for church growth is explained in *Total Church*: 'We are trying to "do church" in a way that is welcoming for unchurched people. We place a big emphasis on sharing our lives with one another and welcoming unbelievers into the network of relationships that make up the church…It is our conviction that the principles we outline can and should be applied to all congregations.'[11]

The authors boldly assert the need for fundamental and sweeping changes in the conduct of churches. The main areas of change involve abolishing reverent corporate worship with convicting and instructive preaching, such as we find in the Bible, the authoritative manual on church life and methods. The typical conservative evangelical church is seen as a company of stuffy, remote people putting on piety. They are, in the eyes of the Porterbrook founders, people who pretend that they are happy, and have no heart for outsiders. A new kind of church must replace this caricature of what earnest congregations have done for centuries. The Porterbrook/*Crowded House* men know better than all who have gone before, their reformation being what they call, 'messy church', with (and no surprise here) worldly music culture.

Tim Chester, in an article entitled, 'A messy church or a pretending church', argues that there are really only two kinds of churches – messy churches, and respectable churches in which people pretend. He writes: 'Life in our congregation is *messy*…Indeed I sometimes describe our church as a group of *messy* people led by *messy* people. One alternative is to be a church in which there is a lot of pretending; in which people have problems, but in which the culture does not allow people to be open about them. Churches like this are very neat and respectable. But I know I would rather be in a *messy* church! Mess reflects, I think, a culture of grace. We pretend because either we do not trust God's grace for ourselves or we do not trust other people to show us grace.'[12]

'Messy church' is a policy of holding church events that are attractive to families uncomfortable with a traditional worship service.[13] A messy church invites people to come for an exciting time of craft, drama and fun, followed by a meal together. But this view is not the scriptural pattern for spiritual worship, for the apostle Paul prescribes that everything in church should be done decently and in order, and especially our worship *(1 Corinthians 14.40)*. Christ gave himself for the Church, 'that he might sanctify and cleanse it with the washing of water by the word, that he might present it to himself a glorious church, not having spot, or wrinkle, or any such thing; but that it should be holy and without blemish' *(Ephesians 5.26-27)*. Such a church strives to be holy, and is not messy.

Total Church is not keen on sermons, which it describes as 45-minute monologues. 'Churches are full of people who love listening to sermons. But sermons count for nothing in God's sight.'[14] The authors like verbal communication to include 'discussion, dialogue or debate'.[15] They like what they refer to as 'God talk'. The apostle Paul commands a different approach. 'Preach the word; be instant in season, out of season; reprove, rebuke, exhort with all longsuffering and doctrine. For the time will come when they will not endure sound doctrine; but after their own lusts shall they heap to themselves teachers, having itching ears; and they shall turn away their ears from the truth, and shall be turned unto fables' *(2 Timothy 4.2-4).*

The overall impression is that *Total Church* is very close to the emerging church movement, sharing also features of seeker-sensitive churches. Like the emerging church, Tim Chester and Steve Timmis promote the idea that traditional Christianity has failed to reach the unchurched and so everything must change. Their new ideas, however, seem far from the New Testament model of reverent worship and the primacy of preaching. And, naturally, their new way of 'doing church' includes all the trappings of contemporary entertainment worship.

Porterbrook and Rap

In 2011 Steve Timmis informed his colleagues in *Acts 29 Europe* that the well-known US rap artist Lecrae was interested in coming to the UK to launch his new album, entitled *Gravity*. Rapper Lecrae also expressed a desire to be involved in an *Acts 29* conference. The Porterbrook coordinator for Cardiff, Pastor Dai Hankey of Hill City Church, Trevethin, Wales, planned both the *Priority* conference and the *Gravity* concert that were held in Manchester in September 2012.

Dai Hankey's blog, entitled 'Sanctified Rant', describes the *Gravity* concert: 'Support acts Cannon, Jahaziel and SO were all fantastic and really got the crowd amped and by the time Lecrae hit the stage the atmosphere at the HMV Ritz was electric! I don't want to bang on too much about Lecrae, because he's all about pointing to Jesus. So all I'm going to say is that I have NEVER seen any Christian musician/artist take to the stage and demonstrate anywhere near the amount of passion, energy, worship and Gospel drive that we were privileged to witness on Saturday night! It was beyond impressive – it was humbling!!'[16]

Highlights from Lecrae's launch party at the HMV Ritz, Manchester, UK, 22nd September 2012 can be viewed on YouTube.[17]

The degree to which the Porterbrook version for the operation of churches has found acceptance among reformed evangelical Christian leaders can be seen from its list of public endorsements.

Rev Vaughan Roberts, Rector of St Ebbe's, Oxford, and president of the Proclamation Trust says: 'The Porterbrook Network is an excellent resource for equipping churches and individuals as we look at responding in a distinctive Gospel manner to the needs in our nation and world.' Dr Tim Keller also gives his warm recommendation: 'The Porterbrook Network is an innovative resource that offers affordable, high-quality training for mission and ministry in the 21st century. I warmly recommend it.'[18] Rev Mark Meynell, Senior Associate Minister, All Souls, Langham Place, London, is equally fulsome in his endorsement: 'It's been very exciting to see how Porterbrook Seminary has evolved over the years into its present form. It uniquely combines a passionate commitment to theological truth with practical missional experience, and so I thoroughly recommend it.'[19]

Wales Evangelical School of Theology

Wales Evangelical School of Theology (WEST), which still presents itself as reformed, evangelical and Bible-centred, joined forces with Porterbrook by announcing the appointment of Steve Timmis, Tim Chester and Jonathan Woodrow to the WEST faculty from September 2013. This new partnership with Porterbrook, according to WEST, demonstrates its passion 'to help equip church planters across Europe'.[20]

Here we should note that WEST has also forged a partnership with SaRang Community Church in Seoul, Korea, which has very substantially assisted WEST financially, taken six seats on the Board of Trustees (including that of Chairman), and made WEST their base of operations for European outreach. The new Korean Chairman is a committed supporter of Dr Rick Warren (having translated *The Purpose Driven Life* into Korean), while SaRang Church is a covenanted partner in Rick Warren's ecumenical and multi-faith PEACE plan. When signing the covenant in 2010, Pastor Jung-Hyun Oh (senior pastor of SaRang Community Church and Chancellor of WEST) said, 'I'm thankful that God has given us this wonderful relationship with Pastor Rick for the past 20 years – trusting one another, walking together…as one team.'[21]

SaRang Church is an 'easy-believism' congregation using the 'Evangelism Explosion' model of calling for decisions. How long WEST will continue to maintain a conservative teaching programme is questionable, with such sponsorship and management, and with a strong faculty element teaching methods taken from the emerging and house church movements.

Acts 29 in Europe

The organisation founded by Mark Driscoll named *Acts 29*, is busy extending the ethos of New Calvinism into the UK. In February 2013 the annual conference for *Acts 29 Europe* was held in Cardiff and given the name *Explicit Conference* after the title of a book, *Explicit Gospel*, written by the president of *Acts 29*, Pastor Matt Chandler, of The Village Church, Dallas.

Explicit Conference speakers were:

1) Matt Chandler, President of *Acts 29*.
2) Steve Timmis, Director of *Acts 29 Europe*.
3) Andy Paterson, Director of Mission for FIEC.
4) Sam Ko, Chairman of the board of trustees of WEST.
5) Elspeth Pitt, staff member of St Helen's, Bishopsgate.[22]

The conference was held at Highfields Church, Cardiff, the organising body being *Acts 29 Europe* in partnership with FIEC. The significance of this conference is that it reveals a network of like-minded organisations that are strongly sympathetic to New Calvinism in the UK. We see the Fellowship of Independent

Evangelical Churches (or at least the leadership), Wales Evangelical School of Theology (WEST), St Helen's, Bishopsgate, the church that founded the Proclamation Trust, and the Porterbrook Network all in open fellowship with Mark Driscoll's *Acts 29 Network.*

7
A Voice From the Past

IN *The Religious Affections*, first published in 1746, the great American theologian, 'Puritan' Jonathan Edwards, warns of the danger of counterfeit religion, which he saw as the greatest danger facing the Christian church, not only in his day, but throughout the history of the church. He wrote:–

'It is by the mixture of counterfeit religion with the true, not discerned and distinguished, that the devil has had his greatest advantage against the cause and kingdom of Christ...By this, he hurt the cause of Christianity in and after the apostolic age, much more than by all the persecutions of both Jews and heathen. The apostles, in all their epistles, show themselves much more concerned at the former mischief than the latter.'[1]

The burden of Edwards' heart was that saints (that is, true believers) should not confuse 'counterfeit religion, and false appearances of grace with true religion and real holiness'. He says that we need to 'learn well to distinguish between true and false religion, between saving affections and experiences, and those manifold fair shows and glistening appearances by which they are counterfeited; the consequences of which, when they are not distinguished, are often inexpressibly dreadful.'

The great folly and heresy of New Calvinism is that it has made no attempt to separate from worldliness. Our response to the onslaught of worldliness must be first to examine every new teaching, and then to expose that which is false. We must understand that one of Satan's greatest deceptions is to mix truth with error. We must earnestly contend for the Gospel of grace once for all delivered to the saints. It is God's will that his people, redeemed by the precious blood of Jesus Christ, should be holy and blameless. The churches of Christ must preach and teach sound doctrine, and encourage godliness and holiness in conduct.

Of course, Christians naturally want to be optimistic when they hear of growth in churches and movements. But it is essential to be discerning. The mainline denominations in Britain have been tragically lost to liberalism because serious compromises were not challenged.

Truly converted young believers have an inborn instinct to turn away from their previous worldly music and dress styles. New Calvinism quenches that desire, and true dedication to a distinctive Christian life. This not only stunts young believers in their Christian life, but brings into the churches those who are not truly saved – causing further spiritual tragedy and troubles in the future for churches.

We are in the world as a soul-seeking people, and we must separate from the things of the world, abstaining from the lusts of the flesh. 'Blessed be the God and Father of our Lord Jesus Christ, who hath blessed us with all spiritual blessing in heavenly places in Christ; according as he hath chosen us in him before the foundation of the world, that we should be holy and without blame before him in love' *(Ephesians 1.3-4).*

The New Calvinist phenomenon described in these pages is a sad story, for it reveals how multitudes of churchgoers have been deceived into following a version of the Christian faith that propounds sound soteriology, mixed with concessions to worldly living. Scripture warns of those who do not teach sound doctrine *which is according to godliness.* Many people, especially young people, have been persuaded to follow a profoundly misleading presentation of the Christian religion, that has appropriated the name of John Calvin and other worthies, to produce inappropriate and compromised behaviour in their lives. The genuine fruit of Calvin's doctrines of grace are seen in believers who strive to obey God's Word, and live holy, righteous lives, distinct from worldliness. The promise of Christ is that he will build his Church. Neither the gates of hell, nor the deception of false teachers, nor the counterfeit religion of New Calvinism, shall prevail against the true Church of Jesus Christ our Lord *(Matthew 16.18).*

Notes

Chapter 1

1 Wikipedia article on New Calvinism, http://en.wikipedia.org/wiki/New_Calvinism
2 Collin Hansen, *Young, Restless, Reformed: A Journalist's Journey with the New Calvinists*, Crossway Books, 2008, p20
3 Ibid. p22
4 Ibid. p24
5 Ibid. p99
6 Ibid. p103
7 Ibid. Endorsements on first page
8 'The Merger of Calvinism with Worldliness', from *Sword & Trowel* 2009, No 1 by Dr Peter Masters, Metropolitan Tabernacle, London
9 *Christianity Today*, 'Gospel Coalition: New group of high-profile pastors seeks return to evangelical consensus', by Collin Hansen, 25 May 2007
10 The Gospel Coalition, Foundation documents, Theological vision for ministry, 'The doing of justice and mercy', http://thegospelcoalition. org/about/foundation-documents/vision/
11 Ibid. 'The contextualization issue'
12 The Gospel Coalition website, 'The Hip-hop Opportunity', Collin Hansen, 10 November, 2010
13 *Christianity Today*, 'Spotlight: Reformed Rap and Hip-hop', February 2011

Chapter 2

1 Timothy Keller, *The Reason for God*, Hodder & Stoughton, paperback edition, 2009, pxi
2 Ibid.
3 Ibid. ppxi-xii
4 Ibid. pxii
5 Ibid. pxiii
6 Ibid.
7 Ibid. pxix
8 Ibid. p223
9 A Special Study of Liberation Theology by George C. Stewart, http://www.thecra.org/Strange%20Club/Member%20Material/AdventuresofGeorge/LibTheo.htm
10 *The Reason for God*, pp224-225
11 Ibid. p192
12 Ibid. p195
13 Ibid. p197
14 David Roy Griffin, 'Values, Evil and Liberation Theology', Encounter, Vol. 40, No. 1 (Winter, 1979), p1
15 Juan Luis Segundo, 'Statement by Juan Luis Segundo', Theology in the Americas, eds. Sergio Torres and John Eagleson (New York: Orbis Books, 1976), p281
16 *The Reason for God*, p223
17 Tim Keller, *Generous Justice*, Hodder & Stoughton, 2010, p6
18 Gustavo Gutierrez, *A Theology of Liberation: History, Politics, and Salvation*, Orbis Books, 1973
19 *Generous Justice*, p7

20 Freedom Torch website, Tim Keller and 'Social Justice', by Jonathan Cousar, 12 April 2011 http://freedomtorch.com/blogs/3/2762/tim-keller-and-social-justice

21 *The Reason for God*, pp 223-225

22 Ibid. pp56-57

23 New Calvinist website, 'Keller's false gospel', http://www.newcalvinist.com/tim-kellers-false-gospel/

24 *The Reason for God*, p87

25 Ibid. pp116-117

26 Ibid. p237

27 Ibid. p240

28 New World Encyclopedia, http://www.newworldencyclopedia.org/entry/Flannery_O'Connor

29 First Things, 'An Interview with Timothy Keller' by Anthony Sacramone, http://www.firstthings.com/onthesquare/2008/02/an-interview-with-timothy-kell

30 New Calvinist website, 'Keller's mysticism', http://www.newcalvinist.com/kellers-affinity-with-rome/kellers-mysticism/

31 Redeemer Presbyterian Church website, 'Meditation: Not So Mysterious', by Jan Johnson http://www.redeemer.com/connect/prayer/prayer_johnson_article.html

32 http://surphside.blogspot.co.uk/2009/06/tim-keller-following-in-warrens.html

33 *The Reason for God*, p93

34 Ibid. p94

35 *First Things*, 'An Interview with Timothy Keller' by Anthony Sacramone, 25 February 2008, http://www.firstthings.com/onthesquare/2008/02/an-interview-with-timothy-kell

36 Deconstructing Defeater Beliefs: Leading the Secular to Christ, Tim Keller, http://www.case.edu.au/images/uploads/03_pdfs/keller-deconstructing-defeater.pdf

37 Freedom Torch website, Tim Keller and 'Social Justice', http://freedomtorch.com/blogs/3/2762/tim-keller-and-social-justice

Chapter 3

1 *Desiring God* website: 'What We Believe About the Five Points of Calvinism', http://www.desiringgod.org/resource-library/articles/what-we-believe-about-the-five-points-of-calvinism

2 John Piper, *Desiring God*, Revised edition, Multinomah Books, 2011, p20

3 C. S. Lewis was not a sound guide, for he had a confused understanding of the Christian faith and much of his writing is deeply mystical. John W. Robbins, having analysed his writings in detail, reached the following conclusion: 'Lewis taught and believed in purgatory (despite the fact that Article 22 of the Thirty-nine Articles of the Church of England describes the doctrine of purgatory as "repugnant to the Word of God"), said prayers for the dead, believed in the physical presence of Christ's body and blood in the bread and wine, a sacrament that he came to call "Mass", practised and taught auricular confession [that is, all Catholics are required to confess all their sins to a human priest], believed in baptismal salvation, and free will. As we have seen, he rejected the inerrancy of Scripture and justification by faith alone, as well as the doctrines of total depravity and the sovereignty of God.' The Trinity Foundation website, 'Did C. S. Lewis Go to Heaven?', John W. Robbins, http://www.trinityfoundation.org/journal.php?id=103

4 *Desiring God*, p21

5 'Sola Scriptura: The Sufficiency of Scripture', Dr Rowland Ward, Part 1, from *The Presbyterian Banner*: July, 1996. http://www.reformedreader.org/ssss.htm

6 http://youtu.be/PDxUw62cRYk

7 Youtube of Passion 2013

8 http://youtu.be/NU0b0yT037w

9 *Christianity Today*, 'Rick Warren answers his critics by Lillian Kwon', Christian Post, posted: Saturday, 28 May 2011

10 John Piper's Regional Conference to be hosted by Rick Warren's Saddleback Church, http://www.carylmatrisciana.com/site/index.php?option=com_content&view=article&id=242:j

Chapter 4

1 http://marshill.com/media/religionsaves/predestination/ajax_transcript?lang=en

2 Mark and Grace Driscoll, *Real Marriage*, Thomas Nelson, 2011, p188

3 Ibid. p192

4 Ibid. p199

5 http://www.challies.com/book-reviews/book-review-real-marriage

6 http://www.dennyburk.com/my-review-of-mark-driscolls-real-marriage/

7 Heath Lambert in *The Journal of Biblical Manhood and Womanhood*, Spring 2012, 'The Ironies of Real Marriage, A Review of Mark Driscoll, Real Marriage'.

8 http://www.youtube.com/watch?v=aVyFyauE4ig, (Driscoll: 'I see things')

9 Donald Miller, *Blue Like Jazz*, Thomas Nelson, 2003, p133

10 'Grunge Christianity?' by John MacArthur, posted on the Grace to You website, http://www.gty.org/resources/articles/a172

11 Driscoll Controversy website, Conduct unworthy of the pulpit, http://www.driscollcontroversy.com/?page_id=289

12 Mark Driscoll's sermon on Humor Part 2; preached on January 13, 2008, http://www.driscollcontroversy.com/?page_id=20

13 Mark Driscoll, *Vintage Jesus*, Crossway, 2007, pp43-44

14 Ibid. p39

15 Ibid. *Vintage Jesus*, Endorsement on first page

16 Ibid.

17 Mark Driscoll, *Confessions of a Reformission Rev.*, Zondervan, 2006, p40

18 *The Radical Reformission*, p126

19 Driscoll Controversy website, Driscoll sees things, http://www.driscollcontroversy.com/?page_id=501

20 Mark Driscoll sermon, part 19: The Weaker Christian from *1 Corinthians 8.1-13* 28, May 2006. Abstract from sermon.

21 *Confessions of a Reformission Rev.*, p25

22 Driscoll controversy website, Driscoll's supporters, http://www.driscollcontroversy.com/?page_id=654

Chapter 5

1 Proclamation Trust website, The History of the Proclamation Trust, http://www.proctrust.org.uk/about-us/history

2 Proclamation Resource Guide 2011/2012, p38

3 Ibid. p41, https://s3-eu-west-1.amazonaws.com/proctrust/Uniflip_Brochure/2011/index.html

4 Music Ministry website, LMMC Talks 2011, 'Culturally Sensitive Music, Andy Fenton, http://www.music-ministry.org/2012/09/lmmc-talks-2011/

Chapter 6

1 Tim Chester and Steve Timmis, *Total Church*, Inter-Varsity Press, 2007, p19

2 Porterbrook Seminary Prospectus, http://www.porterbrooknetwork.org/mediafiles/porterbrook-seminary-prospectus-2012.pdf

3   Porterbrook Learning website, http://www.porterbrooknetwork.org/porterbrook-learning/

4   Crowded House Newsletter, Progress on Porterbrook, Issue 3, 2012

5   Tim Chester online store, About us, http://astore.amazon.co.uk/timche-21/about

6   The Resurgence website, Redeem:Cities Conference, http://theresurgence.com/2010/05/21/redeem-cities-conference-in-belfast

7   Acts 29 Network website, Mission and Vision of Acts 29, http://www.acts29network.org/about/vision/

8   Acts 29 Network website, Leadership & Staff, http://www.acts29network.org/about/leadership/

9   Acts 29 Network website, The Mission and Vision of Acts 29 Network, http://www.acts29network.org/sermon/the-mission-and-vision-of-acts-29-network/

10 Acts 29 Network website, Acts 29 Publications, http://www.acts29network.org/resources/acts-29-publications/

11 Total Church, p19

12 Tim Chester blog, 'A messy church or a pretending church', posted on 16 November 2006 by Tim Chester, https://timchester.wordpress.com/2006/11/16/a-messy-church-or-a-pretending-church/

13 Hope Together Website, 'Messy church for families', http://www.hopetogether.org.uk/Mobile/default.aspx?group_id=132486&article_id=252353

14 Ibid. p113

15 Ibid. p112

16 Dai Hankey's blog, Sanctified Rant, 'Priority + Gravity = Immense Weekend', http://sanctifiedrant.wordpress.com/2012/09/24/priority-gravity-an-immense-weekend/#more-3736

17 http://youtu.be/iGQ6yH_UVh4, http://www.youtube.com/watch?v=RvS36s7rV5w&NR=1, http://youtu.be/LRGUDfjOzG8

18 Porterbrook Network website, Welcome to Porterbrook: College Station, http://www.porterbrooknetwork.org/collegestation/

19 Porterbrook Network website, Endorsements, http://www.porterbrooknetwork.org/porterbrook-seminary/endorsements/

20 Wales Evangelical School of Theology website, WEST Porterbrook, http://www.west.org.uk/porterbrook/

21 http://saddleback.com/blogs/communityblog/peace-plan-covenant-with-sarang-community-church-in-seoul-korea/

22 The Good Book Company website, 'Explicit' Acts 29 Europe Annual Conference 2013, https://www.thegoodbook.co.uk/bookings/details?id=165

Chapter 7

1   Jonathan Edwards, The Religious Affections (1746), Banner of Truth, reprinted 2007, p17

The Dark Side of Christian Counselling
E. S. Williams
155 pages, paperback, ISBN 978 1 870855 65 5

It is amazing how rapidly the Christian counselling movement has spread through churches in the UK, teaching that hurts and depressions once considered part of normal life are illnesses to be treated. It implies that for 1900 years the Bible has been insufficient for the woes of God's people, or for their sanctification, but that now we have the 'insights' of anti-Christian psychologists to make good the deficit.

In this book medical doctor Ted Williams challenges these claims, giving a clear-cut and interesting overview of the counselling movement.

His survey of the careers and teaching of the giants of secular psychology, the pillars of its 'faith', is unique. Nowhere else are these great names so clearly critiqued from a Christian point of view, and their militant atheism laid bare. Yet these are the heroes of new Christian counselling.

Christ or Therapy?
For Depression and Life's Troubles
E. S. Williams
156 pages, paperback, ISBN 978 1 870855 71 6

It is not widely realised that there is an irreconcilable difference between the remedies for sadness and grief set out in the Bible, and those put forward by the world of psychotherapy. A gulf also exists between the biblical policy for marriage, and that proposed by secular marriage guidance psychologists. Many well-known evangelical authors and churches, however, have turned entirely to the secular remedies and policies in these matters.

This book shows what the differences are, including a remarkable review of depression in the Bible, and its relief.

What is Going on in Christian Crisis Pregnancy Counselling?

E. S. Williams

91 pages, paperback, ISBN 978 1 870855 45 7

We hear of very many expectant mothers seeking abortion advice, including girls under sixteen. Dr Ted Williams, a medical doctor of long experience, and a noted specialist in the public health field, shows that Christian counselling centres have adopted a deeply compromised approach which provides non-judgemental advice that leaves in place the option of abortion.

Expectant mothers, including so many girls, should always be helped in a spirit of great compassion, but they must be advised according to the Book of God, and its eternal values.

This book will not only inform and warn, but will focus the aims of pastors and all other Christians when they are called upon to extend help to expectant mothers thinking about abortion.

Do We Have a Policy?

Paul's Ten Point Policy for Church Health and Growth

Peter Masters

93 pages, paperback, ISBN 978 1 870855 30 3

What are our aims for the shaping of our church fellowship, and for its growth? Do we have an agenda or framework of desired objectives?

The apostle Paul had a very definite policy, and called it his 'purpose', using a Greek word which means – a plan or strategy displayed for all to see. This book sets out ten policy ideals, gleaned from Paul's teaching, all of which are essential for the health and growth of a congregation today.

Worship in the Melting Pot
Peter Masters
148 pages, paperback, ISBN 978 1 870855 33 4

New trends in worship have shaken traditional concepts and attitudes, giving rise to much heart-searching and a flurry of books. Is it all just a matter of generation and taste? Are the traditions of today only the innovations of yesterday?

This lively and clearly reasoned book focuses on four crucial principles of worship laid down by Christ and strongly re-affirmed at the Reformation. These central pillars are rapidly passing out of sight today, yet it is surely by these that all new ideas should be assessed.

Here also is a fascinating view of how they worshipped in Bible times, including the Old Testament rules for the use of instruments, and New Testament light on all the elements of worship normative for today.

God's Rules for Holiness
Unlocking the Ten Commandments
Peter Masters
139 pages, paperback, ISBN 978 1 870855 37 2

Taken at face value the Ten Commandments are binding on all people, and will guard the way to Heaven, so that evil will never spoil its glory and purity. But the Commandments are far greater than their surface meaning, as this book shows.

They challenge us as Christians on a still wider range of sinful deeds and attitudes. They provide positive virtues as goals. And they give immense help for staying close to the Lord in our walk and worship.

The Commandments are vital for godly living and for greater blessing, but we need to enter into the panoramic view they provide for the standards and goals for redeemed people.

For other Wakeman titles please see www.wakemantrust.org